BOOK A

Written by Marie-(
Translated by Carly Probert

The Pillars
of the Earth

BY KEN FOLLETT

Bright
≡Summaries.com

**Shed new light
on your favorite books with**

Bright
≡Summaries.com

www.brightsummaries.com

KEN FOLLETT

WELSH WRITER

- **Born in Cardiff in 1949**
- **Notable works:**
  - *The Modigliani Scandal* (1976), novel
  - *The Pillars of the Earth* (1989), novel
  - *Winter of the World* (2012), novel

Born in Cardiff in 1949, Ken Follett is a Welsh writer. After graduating in philosophy, he began a career as a journalist before deciding to write. He specializes in historical and spy novels. His most famous work is *The Pillars of the Earth* (1989), which was followed by *World Without End* (2007). His writing is supported by important historical documentation, which gives credibility to his fictions. With *Fall of Giants* (2010), Ken Follett introduced a trilogy based on the twentieth century.

THE PILLARS OF THE EARTH

WHEN FICTION AND HISTORY COLLIDE

- **Genre:** historical novel
- **Reference edition:** Follett, K. (2010) *The Pillars of the Earth*. New York: Signet.
- **First edition:** 1989
- **Themes:** power struggle, history of England, conspiracy, treason, cathedral

The historical novel *The Pillars of the Earth* (1989) earned Ken Follett his international acclaim. Tracing the history of the construction of the fictitious cathedral of Kingsbridge, the author evokes half a century of British history. To do this, he mixes fiction with historical reality. With his characters, he represents the different sociocultural classes of the time and explores both the religious universe and the secular. The novel was a huge success and in 2010, it was adapted for television.

SUMMARY

In 1123, people witness the hanging of a red-haired man who has been wrongly accused of stealing a chalice. Three foreigners (a monk, a knight and a young priest) stand out from the rest of the crowd. Once the man has been executed, a young pregnant woman publicly curses the three men before running away. This woman is called Ellen, and she will soon give birth to a baby boy named Jack.

Tom Builder constructs a house for William Hamleigh, the son of a local nobleman, so that he can live there with his future wife, Aliena, the daughter of the Earl of Shiring. He is accompanied by his wife, Agnes, and his two children, Alfred and Martha. Unfortunately, Aliena refuses to accept William Hamleigh's hand in marriage and Tom stops construction. William, disgraced, will not cease to seek revenge from then on. As for Tom, he has to get back on the road with his family. He then learns, with both joy and fear for the future, that Agnes is pregnant.

On the road, the family is attacked in the woods and Martha is injured. They meet Ellen and her strange son, Jack. Ellen heals the girl, but Agnes does not appreciate this woman who she believes to be a witch and she forces her family to leave. Agnes then gives birth to her son in the woods, with no help except that of her family, before dying during the birth. Not knowing how to ensure the survival of his child, Tom abandons him in the makeshift grave of his wife. Overcome with remorse, he returns to find him, but he is nowhere to be seen. Soon after, the family comes across

Ellen and Jack again, who say they saw a monk take the baby. Unfortunately, Tom cannot do anything to retrieve his child without confessing that he abandoned him.

Philip, a monk of Kingsbridge, visits the community of the forest and does not like what he sees: the monks do not respect their vows and their lives are far from humble. He therefore takes charge and attempts to change the situation. On the day when his brother, Francis, returns with a baby that he found in the forest, Philip insists that the child be left with Johnny Eightpence.

Sadly, at the same time, the situation deteriorates in the monastery of Kingsbridge and the monk is full of sorrow. Moreover, Francis delivers the bad news of the situation in England to his brother: following the death of King Henry, tensions are high surrounding the succession to the throne that the king expressly left to his daughter, Maud, but that Stephen has seized. A rebellion is forming in order to bring the heiress to power, and Bartholomew, the Earl of Shiring, is one of the conspirators. To protect the interests of the Church, Francis asks Philip to notify the bishop of the Earl's involvement, but, for lack of better, Philip is forced to inform the archdeacon of Kingsbridge, the ambitious Waleran Bigod, instead. Waleran then warns the Hamleighs about the conspiracy. By putting an end to it, they have the opportunity to put themselves in the good graces of Stephen, but also to take possession of the earldom of Shiring and avenge the dishonor that Aliena inflicted upon William by rejecting his proposal.

Tom – who has been hired at Shiring castle -, his family and his travel companions, Ellen and Jack, witness the arrest of the Earl. This is also where the three children meet Aliena. After the attack on Shiring by the Hamleighs, Percy Hamleigh takes possession of the county and Bartholomew is imprisoned in Winchester. When William learns that Aliena and her brother Richard are still in the castle, he decides to go there and rapes Aliena while his companion, Walter, cuts off Richard's ear. But the two victims manage to escape and arrive at Winchester to bid farewell to their father before his execution.

Along the way, Philip and the archdeacon come across Tom and his family, as well as Jack and Ellen. The sight of Ellen clearly troubles Waleran. Back at Kingsbridge Priory, Philip laments his condition and, after the death of Prior James, he succeeds him, with the support of Waleran, in exchange for his help in becoming bishop.

Tom takes his family to Kingsbridge, in the hope of restoring the cathedral. There, he finds Philip and discovers his abandoned son, named Jonathan, in the arms of Johnny Eightpence. However, the priory does not have the sufficient funds for the work. Jack then secretly decides to set fire to the building so that restoration will be considered necessary, allowing his new family to stay in town. Unfortunately, during a visit, the bishop Waleran accuses Ellen of being a witch and everyone finds out that she is not Tom's wife. She is therefore forced the leave the priory with her son.

A few years later, a civil war breaks out between Stephen and Maud who both claim to be the legitimate heir to the throne of England, which is still held by Stephen. William learns of the death of his father, who had become the Earl of Shiring. Therefore, he acquires this title, while Aliena states that the county rightfully belongs to her brother Richard, who then also fights for Stephen.

The Kingsbridge priory prospers and construction of the cathedral goes ahead, despite the pitfalls created by the Hamleighs and Waleran. Jonathan grows up under Tom's nose, without knowing that Tom is his father. Meanwhile, under the patronage of Tom, Jack, Ellen's son, becomes a talented craftsman and sculptor. The attention that Tom gives him stirs a rivalry between the young boy and Alfred, Tom's son, which is reinforced by the budding feelings of Jack and Aliena. After a fight breaks out between the two young men, Tom is forced to fire Jack. However, Jack decides to stay at the monastery to become a monk, despite the disapproval of his mother.

The competition of the market of Kingsbridge is detrimental to that of Shiring and the county's finances take a turn for the worst. William tries to rectify the situation by spreading terror. After trying to prohibit the Kingsbridge market, William leads an attack there that destroys Aliena's trade and causes the death of Tom Builder.

Alfred then persuades Philip to appoint him as head builder to replace his late father and asks for Aliena's hand in marriage. Ruined by the destruction of her trade, the young woman accepts his proposal in order to recuperate the county of Shiring. On hearing this announcement, Jack goes crazy and is locked in a dungeon by Philip. Ellen – who knows of this dungeon because she conceived Jack there with an imprisoned troubadour – helps him to escape. He finds Aliena again and spends a romantic night with her. Despite this, the young woman remains determined to marry Alfred and Ellen curses their union. Jack then decides to go to France to follow in the footsteps of his father. On the wedding night, Alfred is unable to consummate their marriage. Humiliated, he forces his wife to sleep on the floor. Soon after, she discovers that she is pregnant with Jack's child and hides her pregnancy from her husband.

During the celebration of Pentecost in the cathedral of Kingsbridge, the stone vault constructed by Alfred collapses on the worshippers, killing seventy-nine people. Trapped under the rubble, Aliena gives birth to a redheaded child. When Alfred discovers his wife and the baby, he chases them away. On Ellen's advice, Aliena decides to leave and go looking for Jack. After a long journey, she finds him and presents him with his son: they decide to call him Tommy. Jack later finds traces of his father and meets his family.

The three of them return to Kingsbridge. They stage a fake miracle with a statuette of the Virgin Mary and Philip is outraged, until a real miracle occurs. This has the effect of bringing in money and restarting the construction of the cathedral. Philip agrees to Jack becoming the head builder, but requests that he and Aliena, who are expecting their second child, live separately as they are not married. Unfortunately, their quest for marriage is hindered by several pitfalls: Waleran does everything he can to prevent the annulation of her first marriage to Alfred. The situation improves when the latter dies, after being killed by Richard to protect his sister. Their marriage may then take place and Richard leaves on a crusade in order to avoid being arrested by William, who has become the sheriff.

Fifteen years later, the cathedral is completed and Kingsbridge has become a thriving city. At the consecration of the cathedral, Waleran accuses Philip of being Jonathan's father, but Philip is not found guilty thanks to Ellen's intervention. She also reveals that Prior James, Waleran and Percy Hamleigh had wrongly accused and hanged Jack Shareburg, Jack's father, against reward. Jack Shareburg was the only witness of the plot to eliminate the king's son.

Later, the archbishop of Canterbury, Thomas Becket, is exiled for opposing Henry, the new sovereign and son of Maud. However, a group led by William murders the Archbishop. Becket becomes a martyr and the murderer is arrested by Tommy, Aliena's son. As for Waleran, he is named bishop of Kingsbridge. As Richard has been killed in Syria, Tommy becomes the Earl of Shiring and William is executed for his crime. Under pressure from the Pope, Henry repents and is symbolically punished.

CHARACTER STUDY

The characters in *The Pillars of the Earth* can be schematically classified into two opposing groups:

- The first group includes the characters that revolve around Kingsbridge Priory and work on the construction of the cathedral;
- The second group includes those who are powerful and ambitious, work for their own interests and pose obstacles to the construction of the cathedral.

THE KINGSBRIDGE GROUP

Jack Jackson

Jack Jackson is the central character in the novel. A young man, still a child at the beginning of the book, he is raised by his mother, Ellen. They both live in the woods like outlaws. He falls in love with Aliena almost as soon as he lays eyes on her, but many obstacles lie in the way of their love, and even more in the way of their marriage. Thanks to Tom, he learns masonry skills: in addition to being a talented sculptor, he becomes head builder and finishes construction on the cathedral of Kingsbridge, Tom's life's work. As a shy and unsociable young boy to begin with, Jack ends up building a life for himself that many people have dreamed of.

Aliena

A headstrong and stubborn girl at the beginning of the story, Aliena is the daughter of Bartholomew, the Earl of Shiring.

She decides, with her father's support, to refuse to marry William Hamleigh, which leads to him becoming a ferocious enemy. Left to her own devices after the arrest of her father for treason and after her rape, she escapes with her brother and promises her father that they will recover the earldom no matter what it takes. After being ruined she is obliged to marry Alfred, and she gives birth to Jack's child, before going to looking for him. After many hardships, she finally builds a happy family with Jack and their two children. She manages to make her son Tommy the Earl of Shiring, hence fulfilling the promise she made to her father.

Tom Builder

Tom Builder is the father of Martha and Alfred, and is married to Agnes, who dies during the birth of their third child. For fear of not being able to feed him, Tom abandons the baby, who is then taken to the monastery of Kingsbridge. From then on, he is called Jonathan. To accomplish his dream – building a cathedral for the glory of God – Tom abandons a stable job in Exeter and immediately takes his family on the road to look for a new job. Knowledgeable and passionate, when the chance to restore the Kingsbridge cathedral comes up, Tom proves to be a talented builder, but also a qualified and diplomatic leader. His relationship with Ellen, who he meets shortly after the death of his wife, is sometimes tumultuous, but helps him regain his zest for life and focus on his project.

Ellen

Ellen is the mother of Jack. She is the daughter of a rich

landowner, is very educated and speaks English, French and Latin. Her father sent her to a convent, where she fortuitously met Jack Shareburg, a shipwreck survivor with whom she fell in love. They conceived a child while Jack was imprisoned and awaiting execution. Ellen then cursed the men responsible for the death of her beloved, which led to her being accused of witchcraft and having to live in the woods as an outlaw. Later, she quickly falls in love with Tom and entrusts her son unto him so that he can learn the builder trade. Although sometimes over-the-top, she is nevertheless of good advice and, for example, helps Aliena and Jack to be reunited at last.

Prior Philip

Philip became a monk by force of circumstance. On the death of his parents, who were murdered in front of him, he was taken in by a churchman and entrusted to Prior James. He scrupulously respects his monk's vows. Only one sin threatens his faith: ambition. Indeed, Philip cannot hide the fact that he is proud of having become a Prior and he wishes to build an impressive cathedral in his priory. Despite his great goodness, he is very demanding of others, and of himself.

THE POWERFUL GROUP

Waleran Bigod

Father Waleran Bigod is a churchman with burning ambition. Archdeacon in the beginning, he ascends to the position of bishop of Kingsbridge and aims to become the Archbishop of Canterbury after Thomas Becket. This ambition pushed him, several years before, to falsely accuse and execute Jack Shareburg, the only witness of the sabotage of the White Ship, whose sinking caused the death of the heir to the throne. Ellen curses him because of this. It is this story that causes his downfall when Jack publicly accuses him. Waleran ends his life as a simple monk.

William Hamleigh

The son of Lord Percy Hamleigh and his wife Regan, William is a young, impetuous nobleman. He wishes to marry Aliena, who refuses to marry him. He becomes obsessed and, having caused the death of Bartholomew, he rapes the young woman. His obsession still persists and he does everything possible to harm her, as well as those close to her. To achieve this end, he never hesitates to use violence. The attack that causes the death of the Archbishop of Canterbury provokes his downfall, as he is arrested by Aliena's son and executed.

OTHER CHARACTERS

Alfred

Alfred is the eldest son of Tom and Agnes. Unintelligent, his character is defined by jealousy towards Jack, since Tom treats him like a son. Also, they both desire the same woman, Aliena, and Alfred marries her knowing that she doesn't have any feelings for him. He is a relatively cruel man who lets himself be blinded by his own hatred. He is then killed by Richard when he tries to rape Aliena after their divorce.

Richard

Richard is the second child of the Earl of Shiring, Bartholomew. He is destined to regain the title worn by his father. He relies heavily on his sister to achieve his objective and even expects her to sacrifice her own happiness by marrying Alfred to finance his life as a knight. After having killed Alfred to stop him from attacking Aliena, he is forced to go on crusade and is killed in an earthquake in Syria.

ANALYSIS

MAIN THEME: THE CONSTRUCTION OF KINGSBRIDGE CATHEDRAL

Tom's dream of building a cathedral structures the whole narrative and constitutes the main theme of *The Pillars of the Earth*:

- Firstly, it structures the system of characters since most of them are either supporters or opponents of the project. Tom Builder is, of course, its hero, followed by Jack. It is not insignificant that Alfred, who is not presented positively, especially when he forces Aliena to marry him, is the one who, over-confidently, formulates an overly ambitious plan for a stone vault that later causes a disaster and threatens to ruin the entire project. Indeed, following the collapse, construction of the cathedral is halted until Jack takes leadership;

- The construction of the cathedral is also the main stake in the fight of Prior Philip and his companions of Kingsbridge against Waleran Bigod, who is supported by the help of the Hamleigh family. The Hamleighs feel even more involved in the conflict when Percy becomes Earl of Shiring: the cathedral increases attendance to the Kingsbridge market to the detriment of that of Shiring. For William, this also means that Aliena has the opportunity to get rich when he only wishes her misfortune. Waleran and the Hamleighs' attempts to prevent the building of the cathedral range from manipulation and influence peddling, as well as pure violence – the latter at the instigation of William;

- Then, the victories and defeats that mark the progress of its construction always have an impact on the lives of the characters. Among other examples, Tom is killed during an attack by William that aims to stop all construction activity in Kingsbridge and Jack finds his professional accomplishment after taking over the role of he who was his mentor, that of his father;
- Finally, narration generally goes through stages of acceleration during the periods when construction is accomplished without problems. Conversely, the speed of the narrative is slower during the difficult stages, when conflicts are numerous. Undoubtedly, this is due to a desire to sharpen the reader's attention, as well as to the author's wish to convey how a venture of this magnitude progressed slowly and was dependent on the goodwill of those in power and their political struggles.

From the evocation of the bad state of the previous cathedral and its destruction by Jack, at the beginning of the novel, to the final consecration of the Gothic cathedral, this theme runs all the way through the novel and therefore constitutes the main theme.

THE POWER STRUGGLES: THE STRENGTH OF THE LESS POWERFUL

The construction of the Kingsbridge cathedral crystallizes a power struggle. By caricaturing a little, we can consider that this is a struggle between the powerful (the Hamleigh family and Waleran) and the more modest characters whose natures are more temperate (namely Prior Philip, Tom, Aliena, Jack and, for other reasons, Ellen).

The powerful act mainly for their own interests:

- Waleran refuses that funds be spent on the construction of the cathedral because he wants to use them to build a new palace. Gradually, his desire for social success becomes a personal conflict with Prior Philip whose success he cannot accept;
- The Hamleighs join Waleran, at first, because he promises them the earldom of Shiring in exchange for their help, as he had already done to cause the sinking of the White Ship. Once they are masters of the county, they are opposed to Kingsbridge because the expansion of the priory hinders that of their own;
- Meanwhile, William Hamleigh has an additional reason to wish for the downfall of Kingsbridge. For him, this would also mean the destruction of Aliena, for whom he possesses an obsessive hatred.

The other protagonists respond to a more collective interest: the completion of a common project. Unlike the powerful characters, they do not use manipulation to get what they want. It is also significant that when Prior Philip joins forces with Hamleigh to counter Waleran, the result is disastrous since the Hamleighs do not keep their word and forbid him access to the stone quarry.

However, despite the various reversals of royalty that are harmful to the priory, the Kingsbridge cathedral ends up being built and consecrated. Ultimately, it is not the strongest that triumph in *The Pillars of the Earth*.

A HISTORICAL BACKGROUND

The story of *The Pillars of the Earth* contains many references to the major events of the history of England:

- In the beginning of the novel, we learn of the sinking of the White Ship – which really took place in 1120 – and, along with it, the disappearance of the son of Henry I (1069-1135), the heir to the throne of England;
- Throughout the narrative, a civil war unfolds (1135-1153) between the Empress Matilda (1102-1167) – Maud, in the novel – the daughter of the deceased Henry I, and Stephen of Blois (1097-1154), his nephew. They are both fighting over the English crown;
- The end of the novel is marked by the assassination of Thomas Becket (1118-1170), the Archbishop of Canterbury, and the symbolic punishment of King Stephen, also called Stephen of Blois.

On several occasions, Ken Follett mixes small and large history. Thus, the position reversals of the monarchy sometimes favor the construction of the Kingsbridge cathedral and other times, hinder its advancement.

Given this historical backdrop, Ken Follett's novel can be considered historical. The main characteristic of this genre is the mixing of real events and personalities, which mainly serve as a framework to the narrative, with the fictitious facts and characters. In this case, though the historical context refers to reality, as well as some names, the main characters - Tom, Jack, Aliena, Philip, Ellen, etc. - and their adventures have all come from the author's imagination.

FURTHER REFLECTION

SOME QUESTIONS TO THINK ABOUT...

- What are the main disruptive elements that hinder the construction of Kingsbridge cathedral?
- Ambition affects many characters in *The Pillars of the Earth*, in quite different ways. Explain.
- To what extent are there links between the historical narrative and fiction?
- What similarities and differences exist between the characters of Ellen and Philip?
- Why do you think Ken Follett includes historical figures in his novel?
- Explain how the character system works in the novel.
- What are the reasons for the rivalry between Alfred and Jack? Develop your answer.
- In your opinion, why does the action of the novel take place over half a century?
- Episodes of violence are numerous in the novel. In general, where do they come from? Develop your answer.
- How would you qualify the image painted by the author of society in the twelfth century?

We want to hear from you!
Leave a comment on your online library
and share your favourite books on social media!

FURTHER READING

REFERENCE EDITION

- Follett, K. (2010) *The Pillars of the Earth*. New York: Signet.

ADAPTATIONS

- *The Pillars of the Earth*. (2010) [Television miniseries]. Sergio Mimica-Gezzan. Dir. Germany-Canada: Tandem Commnications.
  With the exception of a few changes, the adaptation is relatively close to Ken Follett's works.

MORE FROM BRIGHTSUMMARIES.COM

- Reading guide – *The Century trilogy* by Ken Follett

Bright
≡Summaries.com

More guides to rediscover
your love of literature

www.brightsummaries.com

©BrightSummaries.com, 2016. All rights reserved.

www.brightsummaries.com

Ebook EAN: 9782806270276

Paperback EAN: 9782806271631

Legal Deposit: D/2015/12603/510

Cover: © Primento

Digital conception by Primento, the digital partner of publishers.